AGING AND RENEWAL
Living the Full Life

Michael A. Susko

AllrOneof Us Publishing
Baltimore, Md & Huntsville, Al

AGING AND RENEWAL: LIVING THE FULL LIFE

First edition. September 19, 2022.

Copyright © 2022 Michael A. Susko.

ISBN: 979-8215299364

Written by Michael A. Susko.

Table of Contents

To my friends in their 80s who keep offering their lives and vision to us.

To Dr. Richard Mullin who read my work and complimented he is "aware of the beauty, power, and significance" of the ideas presented.

And thanks to NovOntos for the use of his graphic, *Leviathan*, on the book cover.

PROLOGUE

The quote I've most often cited to others during my life is that of a German mystic, Meister Eckhart. "I'm younger than I was yesterday, and tomorrow I will be younger still." One tends to come up with quotes like this as one ages, perhaps to reverse the psychology that we are only becoming old and diminishing. Yet, there is truth to the paradox the mystic senses. We can experience *renewal* as we age, and unexpectedly so.

In my historical studies, I observed a pattern in civilizations at the 60 generational point. Either the culture rigidified, becoming more set and repressive in its ways, or went through a renewal and openness, typical of the 30 generational point. In the individual life cycle, how sixty years of age, the double of thirty years, can become a re-experience of that youth, is a mystery our society has not recognized or fully explored.

This work argues that the mindset as we age is to not only to age gracefully and minimize the commonplace dangers that occur, but to renew. If we find this key to renewal, we will be able to become a gift-bearer to our friends, family, and larger society.

INTRODUCTION

If we are blessed to live long enough, we experience aging. Certain spiritual developments and dangers arise during this process, for which we may only receive piecemeal information and guidance. We are a culture of the young, and many take steps to deny that we are growing older. But unless we die prematurely, we age.

William James, a pre-eminent American philosopher, said there is no advice to be given. This is true in the sense that we cannot tell other people what to do, particularly if they are not willing. However, life experience and information can be shared. Then, any person willing to listen can then make their own choices. My incentive for doing this work is to help others, even it is a single person on my life journey.

We might wonder, as we go through life, why someone didn't tell us about this or why we did not know something this important. The answer is partly due to *conflict of interest* inherent in our society. Thus, we advocate you read sources which do not have a vested interest or are making a profit from anything you might do based on their work. This is perhaps the biggest caveat. For often, our beliefs are those that the rich and powerful have put in the public domain. If the idea leads you to do things that make you unwell, it will not necessarily matter to those who are profiting. And, if persons do not become aware of certain dangers until they are in the middle of them, they are more vulnerable and will make decisions from which other people can profit.

To find out the full facts and good useful ideas, you will need to read works with no vested interest. Or, you will have to read the original sources in the scientific literature. This has been my experience, that when I went and actually read the medical literature, for example, I found evidence to be much more qualified than people are led to believe. Even then, studies which don't prove what the authors would like to show are often not published. It may be years later when a new meta-analysis study upends the common belief, as, for example, when depression was recently shown not to be due to chemical imbalances related to serotonin.

My goal as a writer, at this point in my life, is to provide as much content as possible, rather than making money. I will not benefit monetarily from choices you might make, but I and others around me will benefit if your life becomes fuller and your contribution to the good increases.

We can start with our bodies and work our way toward issues related more to mind, but the body is always integral to our discussion. This work does not seek to offer specific medical advice on your situation. Rather, it provides more of an attitude or orientation, based on the author's experience and research, which you can incorporate or not. Our basic structure will be to provide five basic orientations and three central areas of awareness to help guide us on how to age and renew.

PART I
CARE OF THE BODY
FIVE EXAMPLES

I am not a Gnostic who thinks the body is bad and should be supplanted by pure spirit. The life we live, with all its array of felt experiences, its sadnesses and ecstasies, is embodied. Thus, it makes sense to orient ourselves to a life that is caring for our body. This is not saying to indulge or make all decisions in the body's favor, but safety and self-care of our bodies are a fundamental to living and aging. It is also involved in renewal.

Our bodies are always regenerating in order to exist. If there is injury, those regenerating forces accelerate. When we go through periods of growth in our youth, the regeneration accelerates as well. As we age, this capacity for biological regeneration still exists, but it takes more time. We must be more patient and wiser to keep our capacity at a maximum for biological regeneration or renewal to occur. Interestingly, our sensitivity to disturbance increases as we age, where body imbalances and sensitivity to pain and toxins can increase. Again, all the more reason for our behavior to be on a curve toward increasing and maximizing our capacity for biological regeneration.

We will now examine five parts of the body as examples that offer problems and solutions in the aging/renewal process. Other areas could be considered, but these are chosen to exemplify an approach. Also, the ready examples offered tend to reflect those areas of our body which have the most direct contact and friction with the world. In each of these, I will feature a personal example to illustrate the focus toward care.

1. *Care for Our Skin*

The skin is an organ on the external surface of our body. It's a truism that it's better to have a problem manifest on the skin in plain view than to have a deeper internal problem. Our skin provides a selective barrier to the world, one that encounters much friction and thus has a high rate of regeneration.

Recently, I experienced a problem with a poisonous toxin around my feet. Clearing sapling in my old Alabama family home, I was exposed to poison ivy. It severely blistered around my right ankle, probably contacting my feet from oils that had brushed on my shoe. It was a bad case and even my dermatologist got a strong reaction from the photograph. My 13-year-old son dreaded to see the leper like condition and acted as if it was contagious.

I had never had such a reaction before from poison ivy. That may have been due to poison ivy becoming more toxic over the years, and also by my body's sensitivity having increased. A Physician Assistant at a party recommended I wait it out. But it burnt like fire, keeping me up at night. Sleep is important because our body specializes in its regenerative response then.

I tried calamine lotion and some older prescription drugs, but nothing was quite working. So, I forwarded a photograph to my dermatologist and called on a weekend. On the advice of the head the practice, despite being hesitant about any heavy medications, I took a 12-day course of steroid treatments to keep my inflammatory response down. The pain immediately ceased. Fears arose, however. A research article just came out that this type of steroid was associated with a decrease of white matter in the brain. However, I surmised, which was later confirmed that this was only a danger for continued ongoing use. So, in this rare case where I take a medication, I limit myself to PRN, or use only for the short term. This is not possible for everyone, but the principle holds: use the least amount of medicine necessary.

As you age, more routine problems will arise with the skin, and they should be tended. The skin reacts to past damage by the sun and may have pre-cancer cells, non healing areas, often around the face. These can be relatively easy to treat by freezing or excising the problematic area.

An oddity about the skin is that it is covered by layers of beneficial bacteria that help keep the natural health of this organ. Thus, too much cleaning, too many additives risk the integrity of this protective bacterial layer. We must be alert that the solution can become a problem. It is necessary to clean to the harmful bacteria away, but too much bathing with soap risks taking away beneficial bacterial.

We can see that in the example of skin, we are already touching upon important principles that will appear throughout this work.

2. *Care for Our Feet*

Your feet are an obvious priority, for they are essential for mobility and endure a considerable amount of abuse over time. The first suggestion about feet is not to stint on having proper shoes. This is particularly true if you remain active in sports or exercise with sudden movement. We are more prone to injury as we age, so having good equipment is important.

Any pain in the feet should be attended and its resolution sought. Walking on the cement floors of Social Services over a few years brought pain to my right arch and a case of plantar fasciitis. The solution, recommended by the podiatrist, was to use hard arch supports, one set of which was specially made for the shape of my foot. This took away the pain. However, in the past few years, my right foot was experiencing reduced feeling and inability to clench my toes. This was a gradual process, but eventually I noted on the tennis court that my foot would feel wooden. That is, I couldn't flex off my foot to propel my sideways movement. There was no pain, just a major limitation of my mobility had set in on the court. I couldn't seem to find an answer for this.

A trip down South where I met up with an old high school friend provided the answer. He explained how he doesn't use arch supports, for they weaken the arch. Along with an article in Consumer Reports which came out shortly after, warning against the use of prolonged arch supports led me to realize that the supports had worked to weaken my natural arch over time. I stopped using the supports and there was very little pain and only discomfort after a long time on my feet. Slowly, the strength has been returning to my arch as it is being used. I can clench my toes now as strength is slowly returning to my arch. Usage is activating the genetic sequencing and muscular response that will enable me to regain fuller mobility.

In this case the solution became the problem over time. The hard supports did serve to control the pain and reduce the inflammatory response in the short term. But at some point, it was no longer needed, and then worked to create a problem. In our analysis of what is going wrong, we tend not to consider past solutions as creating the problem.

This may happen in other dimensions of our life. For example, we might withdraw as a response to social pain or trauma, and that works for a while, enabling self work and healing. At some point, however, this withdrawal is no longer necessary and serves to weaken our social alliances, leading to an unhealthy alienation. The answer to a problem may be simple, right in front of us, and logically deduced. But our intelligence can have huge blind spots, especially when it concerns our body. The solution, in this case, was that I was open to hear comments from a friend, and could also draw the logical inference of how the prior solution was no longer helpful.

Each facet of our body bears a psychological dimension. In this case feet are our grounding in the world, a sense of our connectivity to the earth. It is the fulcrum from which our movement springs. Thus, care of our feet serves to help keep us connected to grounding energies and the earth.

3. Care for Our Hands

Our hands are part of our extremities, which contact the world regularly and directly, with the capability of fine manipulation. We know that the areas of the hands and feet occupy large somatosensory areas of the brain, so the information they collect is of vital importance to our safety and being. Our hands are marvelous mechanisms, a result of an intricate evolution that went through several stages. The evolution of primates, who live in an arboreal habitat and went through at least four major stages, all involved changes with the hands. Such is the complexity and sensitivity, and projecting exposure to the world that it runs a more than usual risk of injury.

A common problem that might arise from our use of hands is carpel tunnel syndrome, pain due to repetitive stress and use of the hand. Over-use and repetitive stressors, without balancing activity, are a common cause of illness and injury.

Our bodies are built for a variety of mobility, and if we limit ourselves to activities which use the tendons and muscles in one way and with much repetition, we will likely have a problem. We will risk injuring the area faster than we can regenerate from the injury. The key is to pace the activity so we can regenerate in time, which can include activities which relax the affected areas. I was a baseball pitcher in high school and college, and after pitching a game, I rested my arm for three days to allow the muscles to repair. This would include soaking my arm in hot water, bringing more blood to the affected area and so increasing the rate of regeneration/ healing.

In the case of carpal tunnel, you want to not only limit the time causing the injury, such as keyboarding, but reverse the muscular pattern. Thus, our hand/palm can be flexed up and toward the body, and you can use the other hand to help pull back the fingers. This stretches muscles not used to being stretched, while relaxing the opposite muscles. Our muscular system is paired to expansion and contraction in different directions, and we must balance usage that goes in one direction.

If we are constantly clenching our hands, it becomes a problem. We have to learn to unclench them. At night, our hands will unconsciously clench, and thus persons may use a brace at night to keep this from happening.

There is a significance to clenching your hands versus their being an open position. In the *orrant* posture of prayer commonly seen in early Christian art, one's palms are extended up and out in order to offer oneself and receive energy from the universe. If our hands are closed and our arms folded against our body, we are shutting ourselves off from giving and from outside energies.

4. Care for Our Teeth

Another area that regularly contacts the world is our teeth. The teeth are the hardest part of our body, the jaw muscles are the strongest muscles in the body, and the whole jaw area is the most evolutionary malleable area of the vertebrate body. The teeth themselves have subtle bumps and grooves which precisely occlude or match with the opposite set of teeth. Additionally, a slight sawing motion by our jaws occurs as we chew our food. The whole purpose of jaws and teeth is to efficiently process food to release nutrients. We would venture to add that this complexity became present to process plant-based materials, as our jaws and teeth came to their evolutionary conclusion. Carnivores, such as alligators, do not need subtle occlusions with their teeth.

Such intricacy requires care, so that our young must be repeatedly instructed to care for their teeth, for our second set are lifelong companions which enables us to nourish our bodies. Regular and frequent enough trips to the dentist are thus a must for our health. We hopefully come to accept and indeed welcome necessary pain or discomfort that care for our teeth involves. It goes without saying that a cavity is an infection in the body and will affect all the organs of the body.

I went through a period in my young adulthood where I felt that a once-a-year visit was too frequent and unnecessary money was being spent. So, some cavities progressed longer than they should have. Now with an excellent dentist, and several crowns on my teeth, repairing that damage, I have come to a better state.

The problem I focus on, which is more ongoing, is one of the jaw clenching at night. TMJ is a condition that refers to the temporomandibular joint. Due to stress or perhaps unreleased anger, the jaws can unconsciously clench at night and grind your teeth. This causes harmful wear to your teeth, and can leave you with a hurting jaw and headache in the mornings. A solution offered which mitigates this effect is to wear a specially formed plastic guard over one set of your teeth which softens the clenching.

There is a mystery as to why the jaws would be a reservoir of stress or emotion which causes this unconscious clenching at night. The whole jaw and teeth area forms an evolutionary and nerve-connected complex in the head, intricately bound with a variety of function—not only eating, but smell, hearing, and speech. This multi-dimensionality means that a lot of currents of energy and information are related to the jaw. So, in one sense perhaps it is not surprising that stress could focalize here.

During this past period of Covid with quarantining, dentists have noticed much more of this clenching/grinding problem. So, perhaps it's safe to say that this phenomenon is related to stress, and the action of clenching seeks to dissipate it. The problem for us is how to allow the body to dissipate stress without injuring ourselves. The mouth guard offers a type of solution. You can also do jaw exercises, where you open the mouth wide, to reverse the clenching muscles.

I think this problem/solution touches upon a larger issue with our whole lives. How do we dissipate the stress of our lives without injuring ourselves or others? What guards, what reversals of energy flow should we put in place, to control potentially injurious expressions of stress release?

5. Care for Our Sight and Hearing

Our head, the most complex area of our body, harbors the key senses. All of them need to be cared for, especially sight and hearing. I will focus mostly on hearing as aging may have its most dramatic impact there. Generally, I do not stint in caring for any corrective means, buying the best or near best products. Our safety and effective interface with the world depend on these senses and they should be kept at an optimum so we can continue to live the full life we had in younger years.

With my sight I have not had any major problems, though some sudden loss of vision in one eye portends a potential cataract issue. This clouding of the lens is routinely corrected by surgery now. One smaller problem that arises is to make sure we wash our eyelids. Oil glands in the eyelashes will clog up and cause sties and inflammation. One other suggestion with eyes, that as we keyboard and look at screens, allow for yourself to have a faraway vision, such as looking out the window or up at a coffee shop. Thus, the eye can focus both near and far and not be locked into one mode.

Hearing is a critical yet often neglected sense with persons who age. There can be an embarrassment to wearing hearing aids, as it identifies someone as handicapped and older. Interestingly, currently aids are quite small and largely unnoticeable. Many people wear AirPods or have some device in their ear that you often have to call attention to having hearing aids, for people to notice them. My main comment though on this score is this: People may or may not notice if you are wearing a hearing aid, but they will notice if you miss a sentence.

Persons generally wait five years longer than need would dictate to obtain hearing aids, and many leave the problem uncorrected. It's a gradual incremental process and you typically don't notice until after you need it. People around you will generally notice first.

Advantages to good hearing are obvious. Your social life, intellectual life, and engagement with the world are maximized. Your risk of dementia declines, as hearing loss is a risk factor for dementia.

Many people resist getting aids due to cost, even when they can afford it. In my view, a high cost that optimizes your interaction with the world is well worth it. In general, we need to improve or up the technology as we age. With just mild or moderate hearing loss, I have fairly high-end aids which cost a few thousand. Again, to me, a price can't be placed on being able to effectively interact with the world, including a son who does not like to repeat things. This aid has different programs that automatically kick in for different environments, such as music or small group conversation. Further, it blue tooths to your phone or television with remarkable clarity. Not all can afford this and social programs should be available for those who need help to obtain good quality hearing aids.

In my case, I went to a local University program which trains students and offered a high-quality service. These services are rendered most effectively in person. If possible, you should avoid the shortcut of buying a cheaper aid online or in a drug store without professional testing and evaluation. If you need ear wax removed so you can hear more clearly, that can't be done over the internet. The latter issue is one that we should not neglect, for over time wax accumulates and needs to be removed by an ear-eye-nose doctor. All this being said, the fact that hearing aids are now available over the counter and are significantly cheaper, is better than no treatment at all.

The alternative to enduring hearing loss without obtaining an effective hearing aid is to slowly drop off from society and become isolated. Everyone around the person notices the hearing loss, but they are often resistant and slow to make the adjustment. Part of this is a denial of the diminishment that is occurring. Denying that aging is occurring does not stop the aging process. We need to learn to accept our body in all its beauty and its fragility, with all stages being part of the journey.

To sum thus far, the general approach to the body should be one of thoughtful care. Don't be a gnostic and make your body your enemy. One should listen to the body as the first step toward renewal.

PART II
FOUR DIRECTIONS TO MOVE TOWARD

There is enough information available to establish what directions we need to move that will amplify our ability to renew and keep our rates of regeneration at a higher rate—in short, keep us healthy. We will highlight just four that have practical implications for how we behave. The hardest thing for humans to do is change their habitual behavior to resolve some issue. The tendency is to look for an easy solution or deny the problem altogether. That is why we frame these as directions to move toward rather than assuming we can arrive there all at once. If we make but a little progress daily, it will add up to become substantial. In the same vein, a small problem that increases daily will become a major problem over time.

1. Toward a Natural, Plant-based Diet with Portion Control

Hippocrates said our first medicine is what we eat. This is reflected now in the movement that would prescribe healthy food as part of medical practice. Many health experts place our diet as the strongest determining factor in whether we lead a healthy life or go down the path of disease. We concur that what we eat is a critical component of our ability to renew and stay healthy. If there is one specific principle clearly established by scientific study and a number of books, it that is healthier to have a plant-based diet. Years are added to your life. Meat should be thought of as more occasionally consumed, a condiment, or excluded altogether. Our teeth, as we have seen, are designed for processing plants. If meat were sufficient to sustain the human race, our jaws and teeth would look very different.

Meat can be seen as a shortcut to substances the body needs. For the short term, it works. But it is harder for the body to process, and the long-term effect is to create a stressor which makes disease like cancer more likely. In addition, unwanted fats clog our arteries and create heart disease. Related to this, as adults, we would be better served by drinking a plant-based almond milk, rather than milk that comes from animals.

To this, we add that we should avoid processed foods, in which additives or preservatives are added, and we can find listed on the ingredient label. Again, the energy to process these foreign chemicals is a stressor to our system and makes diseases like cancer more likely.

Last, we add the phrase "portion control." Not enough food is stressful, but eating too much is also stressful for the body. It is well known that as we age, our activity can decrease and that it is easier to gain and keep weight on. Thus, our direction in eating should be a movement toward portion control. The more we eat, the more we have to process, the more stress that creates on the system.

In this view selective fasting makes imminent sense. Rest a stressed system. Skipping breakfast and extending the night fast is a good step in this direction. Find even small ways to fast, having a salad for lunch without a lot of carbohydrates, and a less heavy dinner. If you are able, substitute bread and water or juice for a regular meal. All these measures point us in the right direction.

In this vein, keeping our weight moving in the direction of losing or not increasing is a healthy goal. More body requires more work by the heart, more food to process to maintain body tissue. Finding one's ideal weight and moving in that direction is a reasonable way to frame our goal. When we eat more plants, such as a large salad, it can leave us feeling filled, versus excessive carbohydrates, which causes weight gain.

In sum, as we consider food, think these three things: Plant-based, portion control, and selective fasting. Don't wait for the diagnosis to make your dietary change. Start now and the positive effects will have sufficient time to have their positive effect.

A counterpart to portion control is something one should do more of when they age in terms of ingestion. As one gets older, there is a tendency to not drink adequate water or other fluids. Of course, one should be alert to minimize high sugar content and carbonated drinks, realizing that any repeated use is a stressor.

I can share a story related to inadequate fluid intake. Once, I was severely sick with bronchitis with a cough that would not stop and made sleep difficult. The whole chest system became highly stressed. When I went to the Patient First office, the nurse took a urine sample, and the color was almost brown. She immediately informed me that I wasn't properly hydrated. Thus, through the distraction of illness, I was unbeknownst to myself, not taking in enough fluids. Of course, dehydration is a needless stressor to add when you are sick! Thus, the color of your waste is informative and diagnostic. Being alert to what goes in our system and what goes out of our system is an important part of maintaining our aspiration to renewal.

2. Avoid Unnecessary, Repeated Stressors

At this point we add a principle that has been emerging, that repeated stressors to our system carry a health risk. Of course, to some extent, living is a stressor, and one can argue we need a certain level of stress or problems to keep us challenged and vibrant. But as we age, we find that the repeated stressors of our life are starting to cause pain. That signal of pain should be listened to and analyzed. What is causing this pain and how can I change my behavior or attitude to mitigate this pain? Perhaps I have learned to not hear the pain or to respond to the pain because that is not manly. Yet pain is present as an early warning system that needs to be addressed before it culminates into a chronic issue or death.

Perhaps the best example of the harm of repeated stressors is cancer. Stephen Hauptman, a cancer researcher and his wife, who headed a cancer institute in Berlin, stayed with me for several weeks while visiting the states. He published a paper, which I helped edit, in *Medical Hypothesis*, "Transposable Elements: Is there a link between Evolution and Cancer?" The basic theory which Steffen explained to me was that cancer is often caused by repeated stressors. That is, the body is always having some errors that could produce cancer, but the system self corrects. However, if the system is being stressed, it is more likely for the cancer to break through. Thus, for example, if you smoke and your esophageal lining is consistently stressed, it is more likely you will have oral cancer. What happens is that the cancer is a localized way to dissipate the stress. While "good" for the short term on the local level, it is bad for the whole organism, long term.

The awareness of the critical component of environmental stressors does not play well into those theories which emphasize genetic defect or mistakes as unrelated to the outside world.

We have already considered how repeated stressors in our areas of the body, such as repetitive movement syndrome and walking on hard surfaces causing fasciitis of the feet, can lead to problems. To this we could add the obvious problems of drug or alcohol dependence, which are by their nature are addictive and so repetitive. With this awareness we are encouraged to find balance, moderation, and if necessary, abstinence in continuing any bad habits we may have.

In his work Steffen cited a paper I wrote, entitled "The Fragility of Evolution." In that work I argued that evolution by its nature is a fragile process and needs to be protected. In the context of this work, aging is a fragile process and we must take steps to protect ourselves and our bodies.

3. Keep Touch/Massage/Gentleness in Your Life

We emerge out of a fluid medium which presses itself all around us, and then we are enveloped by our parents. Touch is fundamental to human existence and is omnipresent when we are young. Although our actual physical contact with others naturally diminishes as we mature, it is still a strong need if hidden need. The impulse to find a partner in an erotic relationship is one way to help fulfill this need. We might say that as we age in particular, we are at risk of "losing touch" with this necessity.

Given the fragility of human relationships and limitations, even of partners, there is another strong way to meet this need and provide a strong health benefit. In our time we have witnessed a movement toward and acceptance of massage in our society as a de-stressor, an expression of nurturance and as a therapeutic benefit. The long list of health benefits from massage is often given from reducing blood pressure to keeping your muscle tone. Massage as a solution with minimal side effects is a preferred choice versus taking a medication which often has side effects which can be risky.

This is one "treatment" that should not be PRN, or taken just as needed. Monthly or biweekly massage build a therapeutic effect from being a regular practice. It is relatively expensive, but what price can one put on their health? To give an example, I have some soreness in my left hip that I noted when I did yoga stretches. However, that discomfort was extending into when I wasn't stretching. Its origin might have been carrying my child on my left hip, even when he was a toddler and weighed forty pounds. After upping the frequency of massage, the pain went away, though I can still feel relatively minor sensitivity when stretching.

Massage carries some risk. There should be good communication with the therapist to adjust the pressure so that the client is not experiencing untherapeutic discomfort. Further, the goal of massage should not be titillation but stress reduction, therapeutic healing, or, as in the case of athletic massage, priming the muscle tone. A sense of boundary is important and one senses when it is crossed. Each person should try to find the right therapist and modalities for their therapeutic needs.

On the other side, we may not do massage because we feel too vulnerable and exposed in that setting. However, from the array of therapists available, one can likely find the right therapist that makes you feel comfortable. Some of this reluctance may be due to past trauma, which massage can actually help you overcome by offering the antidote of healing touch. Of course, massage is not the solution for everyone in terms of their need to be touched. But it is a viable, healing option for many.

I have also used the word gentleness in conjunction with touch. It is important that we have environments that are kind and gentle. They reduce our state of alarm and stress, reducing our baseline tension, and enable us to better go into periods of necessary stress.

In sum, if one wants to keep on a path of renewal, touch should be kept in their life. Especially, a form of therapeutic touch becomes more important as we age, with the need to de-stress and encourage the forces of renewal within us.

4. Keep Symbiotic Modes/Attitudes of Healing in Your Life

There are two basic orientations to medicine and healing. One is to go against the symptom expression and seek to minimize or eliminate them. The other is to listen to symptom expression and seek to direct it in a healthy way. These two approaches are not mutually exclusive and perhaps it is best to think of these approaches as in tension, where sometimes the best approach is to directly fight something. However, a symbiotic or "living with" approach is the one we now consider as a more neglected modality and which holds hidden promise for long-term health and enhancing our renewal. Symbiosis is also one of the great biologic principles which was essential to how life came to be and evolved.

To illustrate this principle in terms of healing, take, for example, the symptom of fever. We can seek to control it, minimize its discomfort, or we can incorporate into our healing approach. Fever, it has been discovered, is the body's way of fighting bacteria, which operates within a certain thermal limit. If our automatic response is to stop fever, we are limiting the body's natural response to heal. Of course, if fever gets too high, in which the body overreacts to the problem, it could become life-threatening, particularly in the young. In this case allopathic medicine, or fighting against symptom expression, is a necessary recourse.

Nonetheless, this example illustrates the principle of first considering the body's natural response as the path to healing. We can see this in psychological problems. If, for example, someone needs to undergo a difficult and radical change in their life, it may be that they will experience symbolic death imagery and/or feel the need to act out some of these impulses in a ritual way. For example, you might lay down for hours with hands crossed over your chest as if you are in a coffin. Such expressions may be frightening to others who don't understand them, but such expressions, if properly contained, may harbor the path to healing.

Similarly, when a virus or plague hits society, the ultimate goal is to "live with" or create a symbiotic relationship with the virus so that is not harmful to the host. This can be done by vaccines which prep the body to respond in a healing way. In the case of corona virus, the body typically overreacted, causing too great of an immune response, which created a host of problems. Thus, a smaller jolt to the system, which also prepared an advance response for a more serious jolt, became a major part of the solution. The virus hopefully does its part too, becoming more attenuated over time, as often happens, and so becomes less likely to kill its host.

"Living with" means that we achieve a balance between taking due precautions and not living in constant fear or over-reacting to a problem. We cannot eliminate bacteria or all viruses in the world, and we would not want to, as they are integrated into our biological systems in beneficial ways. Viruses have also been integrated into our genome, becoming "jumping genes" that add to the dynamism of the human genome and our evolution. Viruses have been tasked by medicine to kill harmful bacteria and thus save lives.

In sum, it would seem that "living with" is a better general attitude or goal than "living against." However, any "living with" must be well-informed and be astute in taking necessary safety precautions.

PART III
THREE EVOLUTIONARY PRINCIPLES AS A GUIDE

In my study of evolution, I have attempted synthetic works of principles based on evidence. In my work *Ten Pulses of Evolution*, I came to realize that three basic categories evidenced a qualitative leap in change. They were:

1.) Consciousness; commonly measured by neural changes/increases and sensory enhancements.

2.) Mobility: The organism's range of movement expands and their complexity of movement.

3.) Social: Changes in size and complexity of social groupings.

These categories are interrelated. For example, primates have the largest, most complex brains of animals, have the widest range of mobility in their arboreal, tree environment, and are the most social of the vertebrates.

Let us take these three principles and apply them to our health and the aspiration to live a full life.

1. Consciousness, Leading Us to Renewal

There is an apocryphal saying of Jesus, "You have heads, use them." In my earlier work on the "Fragility of Evolution," published in World Futures, I look at the principle of the head and whether it is good to have one. After all, a head creates vulnerability. It is so integrated and critical to organisms that having one creates a range of potential problems. Injury readily disrupts the organism, the head demands considerable energy and thus regular food, and its high level of processing needs downtime or sleep to restore itself. Perhaps it would be safer not to have a brain. Some creatures start with a brain, and then lose it when no longer needed, as with barnacles.

This work favors having brains and consciousness. We will assume that you are in the "head camp," that you aspire to have critical thinking, in which you come to your own decisions. Let us consider how consciousness might affect what we have discussed so far. We have already mentioned the principle of listening to the body. Importantly, this listening is complemented by your judgement and your mind. One must decide on how to best direct the body. For example, the body might crave a harmful addiction, but it does not mean that you give no thought to harm reduction or redirecting the addiction. This leads us to consider the fact that ideas often lead to actions that involve tensions between opposing directions. It is something that will all wrestle with and have to come to our own decisions. Hopefully, they are decisions that will nourish the most good in the world.

To do the above, however, we must take time to find evidence and have a reflective mode to consider the evidence. What is evidence and how do we come to accept some evidence as factual? Is it based on a slogan or advertising? Or have we taken time to carefully look at the primary research, and/or consulted with persons who have no vested interest in the matter? Could it be that in some cases, an established expert making a livelihood and profiting from a system with its given set of assumptions should be heeded less than a disinterested friend who has independently researched the issue? This all involves questions of consciousness, the ability to critically think through things and come to the best decision.

What often happens is that there is a lag in our society in establishing the real harm in things. For example, tobacco was much more widely used years ago. Many people were making considerable profit from this product, whose harmful effects were hidden or obscured. Eventually, the evidence about the harm becomes overwhelming and can no longer be denied. However, listening to the body to realize the drug's impact, and the critical thinking that enables us to evaluate its use as a harmful stressor could have led many to give up this harmful habit before the public evidence was clearly established.

This pattern is unfortunately repeated in fields of medicine in which considerable profits are made and evidence is compromised. Unfortunately, we need to incorporate the principle of "patient beware." But to do that, we must develop consciousness capable of rendering a critical judgment. And we must also have a strong enough will to go against the current if need be. Perhaps, in mentioning this, I have stumbled upon a dimension left out, and which is vital to our ability to age gracefully and renew. Let us return to the question of will at a later point.

Let us now return to consciousness and offer four ways to keep ourselves open to receiving psychic methods for renewal. We posit that the universe is giving us, in varied ways and often in subtle fashion, messages that would lead to renewal if followed.

a) Quieting: Perhaps the most direct and most difficult way to tap into renewal is to have some form a quieting that allows things to surface which need tending and action. Often, we have a stream of activity going which has a measure of success and needs little effort to keep going. Even the little spaces for renewal are being filled by stimulation offered by our devices such as phones.

For something new to emerge, there must be a space for it to occur. This can be structured as meditation space, in which you try to do nothing for a 20-minute period. Perhaps you can, in a compromise, keep notes of "to-do" items that surface. Why this is so simple, yet so difficult, has many reasons. One is that we are geared to being constantly productive, and doing nothing is an antithesis. Second, doing nothing is not typically experienced as entertaining. Third, things that are uneasy and troubling within us, that lie just below the surface or not in our immediate consciousness, will surface. In a literary work of mine, *Delphi, the Time Thief, and the Dream World,* I imagine a character being drawn to a Time Expansion Workshop, in which a form of mediation is offered as a mode of time expansion. A paradox presents itself, in which a period of doing nothing expands time. Perhaps, in that period, one enters a zone not constrained by time, which can be referred to as eternity, in which one has an experience not bounded by time. In the context of this work's theme, we hypothesize that the experience of eternity or "untime" renews ourselves.

b) Creative/self Expressions: Another way to access clues to renewal is to do creative activities. Creativity by definition means you are challenged to make something new, or to express yourself in a novel way. When we make something new or uniquely express ourselves, we can then further reflect upon the "image" we have created, in which the work becomes a stimulus to self renewal.

Aging, in a negative sense, can be seen as being in a rut and doing the same things over and over. Being open to doing or creating something new is a sign of youth, in which doors are opened to new ways of being. By doing something creative, we attempt to break through the natural ruts we have engraved upon our lives.

Creativity may be seen as just the realm of artists, something that ordinary people don't do. However, I venture that some form of creative expression, whether it be through conversation, dance, artistic medium, and even the ways which we dress to present ourselves to the world, are all venues of artistic and self expression. If we want to renew or be in the camp of renewal, consider the things that we do which are self expressive, which are honest and come from a deeper place. The artist within us will at least put his or her own slant on the latest fad.

One of the people I have been able to publish is a woman who was in her 90s, in a work titled *DearHeart.* My friend, Brother Jude, had given me this manuscript years ago, and one day I felt inspired to put it out. Decades ago, I had attended a film workshop by her son, who was well known in the independent film making arena. The woman wrote these poems with a simplicity of feeling and directness, filled with little gems of wisdom. One quote stands out in my memory, which resonates with this work. "Keep the spirit of youth, that as we come to look more like a prune, to be like a peach inside." Here, we see the value of creativity in articulating our unique sayings and bringing a sentiment of renewal, which will help us to gracefully age.

c) Listening to Dreams: A major way to tap into renewal, which is little used and neglected by our larger society, is being tuned to dreams. Dreams come from a deep well spring within the self, producing images and a story line which offer us renewal. Last night, for example, I dreamt I was flying a foot or two over a narrow boardwalk over bay waters, the wind passing over my body providing the lift. My arms/hands to either side were tapping the edges of the wood, keeping me within the boundaries of the narrow bridge. The feeling of flight over a potentially dangerous zone, which I am able to control, offers an image of hope and renewal. Though the body's mobility is becoming more limited and our balance is more precarious as we age, there are ways in which we are moving with speed and great precision.

A second part of the dream was focused on a visit to Guatemala, which offered rich images, which I have not fully recorded and are left fragmented. Dreams thus offer images of renewal and hope to us, indicating our strengths. But they also show our weaknesses, what we need to shore up in order to come to the next level. Clues to renewal involve a double work: being aware of our strengths and weaknesses. With all consciousness, there is a call to action to further develop strengths and deal with the weaknesses.

Dreams can venture into the archetypal and outline the stages we've passed through and ones to which we are going. They can provide a map, which if followed, allows new chapters to emerge in our life. You know if you have such a dream for it comes with a certain power. Our life is like a book with many chapters. There is continuity but also newness, which we should be open to and allow if we are to have an interesting book or life.

d) Messages from Others: The universe is humble and may not give you a dramatic vision or dream, but simply a word from another person. This person with a message for us may be someone unsuspecting. It brings to mind a story from one of my brothers. Someone helped him, and my brother offered a five-dollar tip. The man held up his hand and said, "Don't take away my blessing." The message here can be that money has its limits as to the good it can confer, and there's something greater than that which the man referred to as blessing.

One of the disappointing experiences I have as I age is how others may close themselves from me, for whatever reason. I think to myself, but what if I have a word for them that they need to hear? Now, they will not hear it, and that clue to their renewal is lost.

In sum, a general attitude of being open to experiences and messages, whether they come from quieting, creative expressions, dreams, or unsuspecting others, is a key to our renewal as we age. These four "openesses" sounds basic, but if you consider it carefully, each one is uniquely difficult. The ability to renew, to become new again, as we live longer, is not without challenge or work. Yet, it is accessible to us if we dare to risk our current self. Thus, the saying from scripture: those who lose their selves will can gain their selves. Put another way, the willingness to give up or let go of our current self allows us to renew and be young again.

2. Mobility: Keep Movement in Your Life

A second great principle regarding biological systems, evolution, and having leaps in consciousness is movement. If Descartes said, "I think, therefore I am," the dancer in us would say, "I move, therefore I am." Movement is inextricably wound up into our animal being. If you photograph a bird on a tree limb, you will notice that they are rarely still, even if they are perched. There is constant swiveling, their gaze varying. Our view of the world is dynamic with many lenses, shifting between close ups, panoramas, and distance seeing. We can add to this our bodily movement of location and manipulation of things with our hands that alter the world. Movement is essential to our daily activity and only when we become disabled in some way may we realize its importance.

At the risk of stating the obvious, the principle is: Keep movement in your life. It provides a dynamic flow of information that keeps our consciousness alert and tuned. The shaman may experience altered states of consciousness, but he or she often does this through dance and song. The scientist has a theory, but goes out in the field to test it, to see what happens under varied condition.

Movement entails mystery and pleasure. Of the greatest pleasures in life which the Spanish philosopher Ortega e Gasset lists, many are related to movement. These include racing, dancing, and hunting. We love to move, so let us keep movement in our lives. Movement activates sets of genetic activity that go deep in our being from our earliest childhood. Thus, by moving, we are tapping into youth. Yesterday, I mentioned to the tennis pro at the local clay courts an advantage of tennis: "On the court you forget how old you are."

Often, we are instructed to keep exercising, to have some regimen that makes up for muscle loss, that keeps our cardio going. Everyone should find their preferred way. For me, I prefer to be tricked into exercising. In my case, it's chasing after a ball, and whacking it back and forth with another person. Tennis is not my only form of exercise, but it's fun and provides benefits on many levels: tuning hand eye coordination and reflexes, practicing my balance, and giving my cardiac system a workout. One tennis instructor of many years told us that "You live seven years longer if you play tennis." It's a good sales point, but it points to a truth too.

Often, new information is coming out often on the benefits of exercise and how to achieve that benefit. For instance, a day marked by longer periods of sitting with regular exercise of a thirty-minute daily period may not be enough. During the day, we need interspersed periods of movement. Another insight is that maybe thirty minutes for a period of exercise is not always enough. Once a week, a friend suggested that you should weekly do 2-3 hours where you "beat yourself up," extending your normal limits. Once, when climbing long mountainous terrains in Guatemala, I became aware of how much I could press my limits. The feeling arose that we need to press our system sometimes so that we can return and handle the baseline much easier. Of course, we need to keep in mind stories of a person who goes out one day in the winter, shovels snow intensely and has a heart attack. Thus, the caveat to this suggestion is that we more slowly build ourselves to being in shape over time before engaging in an activity that might press our limits. And of course, all suggestions of exercise are age adjusted, to where you have a sensitivity and awareness of your body tolerance and know when to stop.

My Dad played softball even into the last year of his life at 92, for the *Young of Hearts* NASA team. Although others would run for him, he could still hit. Periodically, the newspaper would do a feature about his long active life. We should continue to exercise as long as we can and as much as we can as we age. We should also be open to new forms of exercise. My father did these *Fountain of Youth* exercises, invented by Tibetan monks. Recently, my brother who had recently started these exercises, recommended them for keeping the chakras of all your bodily areas in balance.

When we are young, we incorporate movement into our lives naturally with play and sports. But middle age comes, we get busy and exercise may drop off. Often there can be some injury which discourages us and restricts our movement. It is a subtle balance between protecting ourselves, making sure we have time to heal, but to resume when we are able, so we do not fall out of the pattern of exercise and exertion.

It is a paradox that exercise, which is tiring and can cause injury, is a prime source of renewal. In studies of depression, forms of therapy, were compared. When regimes of drug treatments, going to therapy and having regular exercise, they found that exercise had the most beneficial effect. This suggests that experiences of well-being and a youthful joy are a natural benefit of exercise. Feelings of depression are the opposite of feeling of renewal. If we are depressed, we feel we are stuck, that we cannot change, that we are "old." In short, doing and moving the body has the power to generate good feelings. I would argue "Movement first," as the therapy for our lives, one which enhances our capacity to renew and become youthful.

One final note on exercise, which I credit to a good friend from Alabama. Where we exercise may be important. Research has shown that "forest bathing," walking in the forest results in positive secretions within the body. My father was a believer in the beneficial effect of positive ions in the air, which is felt stronger outside. The positive and exciting energy in the air before a storm reflects this positive ionization. So, in our renewal, let us seek to go outside and immerse ourselves in the local clime, whether it be forests or desert lands.

3. Social: We Renew Through Each Other

When I was in graduate school, I had the good fortune of having a class by Dr. Jim Lynch, who wrote a book entitled *The Broken Heart: The Medical Consequences of Loneliness.* In this work he documents how those who are more socially isolated will live shorter lives by years than those with strong social bonds, which often involves living with others. He also cited the famous long-term Framingham study regarding heart disease, which showed the importance of the social dimension even over other factors like diet and exercise.

This points to an essential paradox, that deep down we live for each other. We see this sometimes in spouses who die closely together. We are taking care of ourselves, not just for ourselves, but so that we may be there for those we love. In my case, a strong incentive to living longer is to be there for my son who is a half century younger than me.

We are often stimulated to gains in consciousness and keeping up with our mobility because of our social connection. Listening to others transfers awareness first hand, which I have already mentioned often relays critical messages to us. Playing a sport together with someone can drive us to exercise much more than if we were by ourselves. Thus, the social dimension can be seen as the key that unlocks our capacity for renewal. *We become young together with others.* The dictum "to love neighbor as self" shows how the two are inextricably bound. In caring for myself, I care for others. In caring for others, I care for myself. Things we do that strengthen the connection with others become a source of renewal and keep us young.

The social dimension is embedded in our evolutionary history in a major way. No life is isolated. The first organisms, known as procaryotes or bacteria, are mounded, expressed in colonies or films. More complex cells are symbiotic consortiums that have tapped into each other to heighten their dynamism. When we go all the way to primates, we note that their social modality is so intense that we have unexpectedly multiple leaps in consciousness.

At this point, a conundrum comes to mind. The path of evolution which favored consciousness has sacrificed longevity to some extent. Lifespans have shortened from the earliest organisms and earliest animals. Procaryotic organisms can survive for hundreds of years and some are believed to have a 250-million-year lifespan. Sponges can live for hundreds or thousands of years. There are jellyfish which appear to live forever.

The goal of "evolution" in terms of the human path, however, is not just to live long, but to have more consciousness. Put another way, longevity has been sacrificed for consciousness. This being said humans have a good life span compared to other vertebrates. Fish usually live only one to ten years, although some live to 200. Smaller mammals, such as dogs and cats, generally have shorter lifespans than humans.

While this work aspires to encourage longevity, it is also focused on renewal. The quality of our years is of equal, if not greater importance, than living long. Renewal implies a growth in consciousness and energy to live out that consciousness in terms of our mobility and our social connections.

Returning to the social dimension, we can reflect that it exists on varying levels. There are one-on-one relationships, small groups, and larger group connections such as churches. Each one is vital in its own way. During COVID we might have found small groups suffering, and that we needed to do things to restore their presence in our lives. There are also social rings around us, from family to street neighbors, to neighborhood, to city, state, country and ultimately the world. Our relationship and connection to each other needs to be checked for its health and what we can do to further it. I will give one example. Through Child Fund, I help support three children across the world, around my son's age. Our family includes an African child, a Central American Child, and an Asian child from the Philippines. I ended up doing this largely for my son, encouraging his connection to other children around the world.

The goal of the social dimension is to keep expanding the circle of love, to warm the dark places of the universe. In doing so, we bring unexpected richness to ourselves and others. And one of those riches is that our being is renewed through acts of love. For love, which I have only touched upon, is ever young and brings the power of renewal. This happens in our writing, our reflection, and our lives. We discover love again, and how it is the source of much we seek.

PART IV

A QUESTION OF WILL

We may have the best advice in the world. We may know what to do. But we don't do it. Old habits are hard to change. The structure of our day doesn't permit or easily invite change. Social pressure may go in the opposite direction. Following the beat of your own drummer may appear foolish.

The reasons we don't do what is good for us and what would enhance our full life is a mystery. Some of it has to do with "legacy," our inherited patterns or electrical fields which "naturally" steer us in a certain direction. To undo or push into a new direction, to break a pattern, requires effort and courage. Yet, to renew and live the full life, we will need to exert our will, to move in the direction that is more life-giving.

Thus, I will try to offer some clues on how to exert the will. Perhaps they will stand out as common sense to anyone who reflects on them. But it is important to set what should be common sense into clear statements, which can settle deep into our being as a touchstone to action.

With this in mind, I offer five suggestions for exercising the will in a new direction.

1. Be Aware

It is critical to be aware. We must face facts as much as possible, as to what is reality regarding the body and the environment around you. This work has been focused on the awareness dimension. Often and surprisingly, it is hard to see what is in front of us. We may have the expectation of seeing X, yet we are looking at Y. Despite Y being there, we still see X and respond as if X was there. Such is the power of human expectation and mind upon our reality. We may, for example, view a janitor as lowly and one from whom we should not expect much. Yet, as a popular Netflix series showed, he may be the person who first teaches chess to a child who becomes a world champion.

Children have a natural gift of seeing what is there, compared to adults whose expectations may keep them from an accurate perception of reality. We often ignore information that our ideas are not accurate or working very well in reality, such is our stubbornness in holding on to our expected perceptions. Ultimately, of course, reality collapses around those who have a false view, and either they belatedly adjust to survive, or remain rigid to the end until their demise.

Advertisers know that awareness is critical, and devise ways to expose us to information such that we will remember it and act upon it. Those in state systems who vie to control others are experts in propaganda. They know that it is important what we read and see and so they try to control those inputs. When you read something, you might ask who had the power to put it there? Does this power have a vested interest in you believing X, even though X may be destructive to you and the world? It may be errorless technically, have glossy photos, but the information it conveys may be false and move you in the wrong direction.

This leads us to consider the direction our awareness takes us, our next clue.

2. Move Small in the Right Direction

We must have an accurate awareness to move in the right direction. Moving in the right direction is of the essence. A saying to keep in mind here is that it is better to be a private moving in the right direction than a general in the wrong direction. To move in the right direction requires a spirituality that is humble enough to risk being small in our movement because it is the right way.

Once we are moving in the right direction—no small matter!—we allow that the steps may be small. Rome was not conquered in a day, and neither will the construction of good habits that overcome our bad habits. William James, the American philosopher, said to put good habits in place by the time you are 30 years old, for after that they are hard to change.

But we are asking those who are twice that age at 60 or more to form new habits, or to amplify habits which would be beneficial to us. It's a seemingly impossible task, yet one we are attempting. Even if we make a change that has only a 1% impact, it is possible this "seed" will, when fed and watered by other inputs, become a larger wellspring in our lives.

One measure of hope is that repeated, small things add up. A right direction over time becomes a qualitative change. We find ourselves changing, becoming different and better despite ourselves. Our new behaviors and actions work to change us.

Unfortunately, this can work in the other direction, in which bad habits amplify and become more destructive over time. Thus, we must watch the pattern and be ever alert to what is happening with ourselves.

To see ourselves accurately is perhaps the ultimate challenge. Ancient philosophers knew this and gave the dictum, "Know thyself." Writing an autobiography is perhaps the hardest genre, for the experiences are so close to us that it is hard to keep perspective and to become overly immersed in our experiences, with all their heights and traumas.

Even though this clue alerts us to the potential of small changes, we do not rule out big changes in later life, for indeed they can happen. Often, just like in youth, they are dramatic and raise fear in those around us. These "breakdown" experiences, however, have the potential for breakthrough.

For now, however, we are focused on the small, on becoming aware and taking steps (rather than leaps) in the right direction. This leads us to the next step, which is to form new habits.

3. Forming New, Life-Giving Habits

It is well known that if you do something repeatedly, say twenty or thirty times, that it can form a new habit. It means the nervous system, the genetic pattern of sequencing involved, becomes activated and are remembered, becoming easier to do next time. It is an important life survival trait. I don't have to think about locking the front door each time I leave the house, for I automatically do it. It may be, however, as I age, I forget I have done it and go back to check. But almost always I have done what habit directed me to do.

Putting in place healthy habits should be part of our repertoire for living. This requires discernment. You start to do something new, and feel pleasure and a warning sign. You make a snarky comment that puts someone down. This comment could move from being occasional to becoming habitual and end up interfering with your social connections. When we do X, we could reflect and project what will happen if we keep doing X and what will happen if that change accelerates and becomes X squared. Something could quickly become really good or really bad. Thus, we need to become alert to the formation of habits, good and bad.

To live a life fully, to renew, we must place ourselves in the business of ever improving and developing our good habits, within whatever limits we find ourselves constrained.

4. Spirituality and Prayer

It turns out that spirituality for all its focus on heights and otherworldliness has a special skill in leading people to do things. If the balance of things, the fate of our soul and the world, depend on what we do, then there is a strong incentive to act. But more than this, when your spirituality focuses on love, actions will naturally flow.

Often, we may not want to do what we should do, or what our spirit is urging us to do. Recently, I did not want to make the long journey south, some 800 miles to see Brother Jude, who is in hospice at a monastery. This artist friend of some fifty years has blessed me with his graphic work, which I use on a lot for my book covers. I knew it is more important to keep making this journey while he is living.

So, I went and had several important experiences that enriched my spirit. To cite one, it was at his insistence that I visited a remote area in Alabama, where a caretaker at the monastery infirmary lived. She collected rocks with Indigenous connection for her, and since I had just published about a stone on the Shenandoah River, Jude thought I should go. At Penn Bluff I came upon a remarkable stone formation that conveyed an anthropomorphic feel and form, which I have since published about. The Universe opens new experience to you, but you must be open to love and acting upon love.

How is that we decide to do the best thing when we don't want to? I give credit to prayer that is often a hidden prayer. Perhaps I prayed for the strength to make this decision—I don't remember—but even if I didn't, I imagine the prayer was made for me. Perhaps, in view of this, though, we need to make an inventory of our "hidden prayers." What re the things we desire and need for our betterment, which are not yet conscious to us?

Still, with this in mind, it is good that we become conscious of our prayer, what we wish the universe to bestow upon us.

PART V
LOVE AND RENEWAL

I have a friend I made while visiting Panera's coffee shop in the afternoons before picking up my son from school. When I first met him, he was writing a book about love. He went away for a few months and when he returned, his project has stalled. There is so much to the book he tells me it would easily be three or four hundred pages. I encourage him to finish it, or settle for a briefer version. My friend is insistent that it needs to be long, and I wonder if he will ever finish it.

You can never write or reflect about love too much. It is a safe touchstone to ever return to and expound upon, to explore its mysteries. So important is love that it is a revelation of one of the world's great religions, that God is love.

1. Daily Acts of Love

Today as I write this at a Starbuck's coffee shop, I see a young African American sitting outside the shop under an awning. A heavy rain is pouring down a few feet away, the remnants of a Florida hurricane. A habit from my days as a Homeless Outreach Worker, I approach him and offer a few dollars, which he accepts. Enigmatically, the man tells me he wants to become a Native American. I respond, "That's a worthy aspiration." He's outside in part because he's preparing to smoke some weed, which he has me smell. He looks at me and says one day he wants to be old like me, to sit in a rocking chair with a friend, and tell stories. I relate to this and add, "And new stories will keep happening."

Here is an example of reaching out to someone, in which the man—it always seems to be a surprise—offers back a gift, a richness from his being.

Love and the opportunity to love are all around us. Love is a portal into new experience, into surprise, and into a warm world. I dare add that love is also a portal into eternity, in which an experience becomes enshrined forever into the memory of the universe. For no act of love is ever lost. The man did not know I was writing on aging and renewal, yet he has added his statement to this work.

On the same day, in the afternoon at Panera's, I sit by an African American gentleman, who revealed he is 84 years old. He was not looking at a phone or computer and seemed like someone open to meeting another. I share about my book project on *Aging and Renewal,* and he immediately directs me to a scripture verse in 2 Corinthians 4:16: "Though outwardly we are wasting away, yet inwardly we are being renewed day by day."

Curious, I looked up the Greek word for renewal used in scripture, and find that it is *anakainoutai,* which translates as "is being renewed." It is a particular form unique to Paul. I kid my new-found friend, as I do my son, that I too have a literary license, that I can make up words or variations of words. So here is an important clue: our Inner Being can be renewed, despite the fact that we face bodily diminishment. An interesting paradox emerges. As we get older, we have had more days to be renewed, and in a sense, can grow younger. The number of times you have experienced renewal can be seen as a measure of your youthfulness.

Last, I mention something that was significant to my becoming aware and tapping into "daily acts of love." My brother John wrote daily spiritual letters to our mother and father, which often reflected on the beauty of nature and which I published in *Flowers of the Night.* After he passed, I continued the tradition for three to four years, now doing them occasionally. What I have found from my daily writing is that every day is rich in beauty and opportunities for love. Each day is a marvel, if reflected upon. And most interestingly, all the acts were held together by a subtle spiritual thread, which created the title to the letter, and whose theme inevitably relates to the myriad expressions and ways of love.

2. Renewal at Sixty

At thirty years of age, we enter history and impact the world. We have established our basic vision of the universe back in our early 20s, and we are now ready to influence things more than be influenced by them. In my study of history, I found the 30th generation of a culture (in which generations are 15-year increments) is when the country had consolidated its identity, and become strong enough to open itself up to outside points of view and influences. It was a period of light which largely operated under the influence of positive spiritual forces. Rome built the world-embracing Pantheon during this period, and the medieval era built its Gothic lightscapes.

But what happens at 60? We have gone through the 40s where we challenge those who have power in the world, who are often in their 50s. For me, I see this as a challenge to begin a new chapter in life, in which one offers their vision to the world, in which one is mentoring others.

Our society pictures the 60s as one of retirement and, if you can afford it, time for long cruise trips to exotic locations. But retirement from a job which gives monetary compensation is not an end state, but a door through which we pass. It signals a new chapter, which we will write. One theory of how human evolution was ignited is that humans began to live long enough that grandparents could help in child rearing. This bond between grandparents and child is a formula for renewal. For the grandparent, in close association with a child, renews. The child experiences the renewal of someone free from the busyness of the work world. My 13-year-old son has told me, "Dad, you are old. You are really old." But he will also say, "Dad, you still act like a kid."

In short, keeping children or youth in your life is a key source of renewing as we age. Children open up the doors of love and with love we renew.

3. Meaning and Projects We Love

My wife knows I am writing this work, and she added the comment, "Have projects you love." To find one's love as we do things in the world sounds like a worthy goal. I have had an aesthetic streak, where I do things for their value, not focused so much on whether I love them. Being able to accept and recognize our loves is an important part of living the full life and renewal toward that end. I think I am just coming to that full awareness now.

In my life, I have enjoyed discovery, finding new patterns or resonances in the world. But whether our discoveries are novel to the larger world or not, we need to be on the path of discovery for ourselves, to see things through our unique lens.

Perhaps even more important than the thrill of discovery is the creation of meaning. I had the honor of Viktor Frankl writing me after I sent him a book, *Cry of the Invisible: Writings from the Homeless and Psychiatric Survivors.* He wrote the famous book, *Man's Search for Meaning,* in which he discovered that in the depths of the horrors of the concentration camp, the search for meaning was still critical and ongoing. I found too in stories I collected, that even amid the despair of homeless and breakdown experiences, meaning emerged. One can even make the case that the density of meaning logarithmically expands during these crisis phases.

This leads me to say that those who experience depth of meaning in their lives tap into a strong source of renewal. Something that our being loves do, renews us, makes us feel alive, and signals our own importance.

PART VI
TOPICS SO FAR OMITTED

As I come toward the end of this work, I find there are things I have approached but leave out or mention only in passing, even though they are essential. What we leave out, what we find more difficult, are often the more important areas we need to focus upon in terms of our development. They can be areas of weakness with which we can make the most progress.

1. Offering Our Failings as a Pearl

A quote I have found useful is one by Pope Francis, which I paraphrase, to offer our sins or failings as a pearl to God. If we are on the path of actualization, of becoming more loving humans, we become acutely aware of things, large and small, that get in the way of that path. They may be habits that dissipate our life energy or *chi,* such as overuse of alcohol. We know what these dissipating forces are and we need to exert self control. However, we fail. I remember a quote from a homeless man, something to the effect that we wash off last night's mess and experience the brightness of morning.

We are not going to avoid failings in our life, but we mustn't let these failings define ourselves and keep us from the path of doing good. We offer the failing up, what good there is in them, and let them go. We don't have time to become self-absorbed in them, particularly as we are older, because we have good to do this day.

We also offer our failing as a pearl because our love for ourselves is deeper than any hate or disdain we may have. Somehow, love is able to transform our failings. How it does that is a mystery that remains to be explored.

2. Acceptance of the Body and Its Workings

We are not Gnostics who believe that the body is the enemy. We should, as we age, come into a fuller acceptance of our body to accept the blessings of having its parts working. Interestingly, experiences of pleasure we have with the body are experienced in the mind. But if we do not allow the full experience or try to shut them down, we are repressing the body. Thus, to be in harmony with the body, the mind must allow the body to have its experience.

One can make the argument that the ecstasies we experience in our youthful bodies will not necessarily diminish as we age. For if our mind and spirit are more in harmony with the body, the gift of the body will continue. Our body's sensitivity increases as we age, where we feel acutely if we step on a small object with our bare feet. Likewise, our ability to experience pleasures and joys can acutely increase. Be open to this paradoxical expectation and see what happens.

I remember interviewing the psychiatrist John Weir Perry, who studied under Carl Jung, and whose history I published in *Transformative Experiences*. He was in his 80s, and as he got up, not without some resistance from his body, he said, "I don't believe in this aging stuff." I think the meaning here is not to be hemmed in by the false expectations of aging, that we are just growing old, and that we cannot renew and become young again.

3. Acceptance and Control of our Sexuality

We have just reviewed how experiencing the fullness of our body is integral to our humanity. This includes the sexual nature of our being. Our sexuality can blossom even as we age; it may lessen in some ways and become more acute in others. This is a complex topic which is historically conditioned on our experiences, good and bad. I don't pretend to be a guru in the matter, and I am naturally shy about such discussions. But questions involving sexuality don't disappear because we age. Here are some working ideas, often from sayings I heard from others, that have helped guide me in this area.

The first, already mentioned, is an acceptance of our body, the goodness and gift of sexuality. It creates interest, makes for a dynamism, drawing us out to give ourselves to another. Inherently, it is a beautiful thing. It calls to mind my relationship to an elderly woman in her 90s who had no relatives left in the world. I was much younger at the time in my 30s when I visited her. Occasionally she asked for light massages which I was able to do for her. She spoke about her sexuality, which she still felt present, and how a priest had told her that it was a gift God had given her. In the end it was only me who was left to help bury her. She had rights to be buried in Gettysburg, atop the grave of her husband, a WWI veteran.

Sexuality is part of the fabric of creation, and it has a wide variety of expression. The variety is hard to keep in mind or give it its due when we are focused on the full expression of erotic love. The celibate lifestyle, which I lived for many years, has a type of generalized sexuality in which subtle expressions of love can be felt acutely. It can be a valid form of sexuality, even though society may not understand that.

There is a paradox to sexuality. C. S. Lewis believed it was a beautiful gift, but one that can be easily abused. The deepest expressions of sexuality involve such intimacy and emotional bond that it should not be casually tossed about.

I remember taking a walk with a priest who was the head of the Sulpician order, who taught other priests here in Baltimore. He said, "There is a pleasure in denial as well." Sometimes to fast from something serves to rest our system, but can also increase our appreciation for the thing denied. Paradoxically, our ability to deny pleasure is woven into our ability to experience pleasure.

Another saying in a conversation that stood out was from a wise woman who was in the healing arts. She said that alcohol and sex absorb *chi*. The message here seemed to monitor things and be careful about overdoing them. That is, we are making decisions all the time about where to put our life energy. That energy is not unlimited.

It seems that our working ideas often involve tensions between opposites. We know that sexuality is a good thing, and that it needs to be controlled, as it can lead to trouble. We want sexuality to be channeled within our being so that it furthers our life's direction, not pulls us away from it.

Sexuality is complex, in part because past traumas can be associated with it. If this has happened, and often it has, we have wounds for which we are seeking healing. This calls to mind once when I was a small child and a babysitter hit me hard in the upper leg for some reason. Now, when I am massaged there in a gentle way, I might recall the event embedded in my body's memory, and find the current touch to be healing from this past event.

Wounds from our past bring the danger of steering us toward non-acceptance of our bodies, of blocking avenues of the body's natural expression. How we go about finding that healing is part of our adventure with sexuality. Ultimately, we are looking for loving ways that are healing to one another.

Perhaps there is a life force, this *chi,* that naturally flows from us. One current in this is our sexual being. For the rainbow that is ourself, we need all these currents flowing together. That is, our bodily being with its sexuality, our psychological being with all its emotions, and our spiritual being with all its high aspirations should come together to maximize our loving presence in the world.

I had a conversation with my brother earlier this morning, who described how his ability in law has grown such that he can now see quickly the whole picture and discern what is important in a case. Our synthesizing mind increases as we age. I would like to think too that our synthetic being can increase as we age. Put another way, our "holistic" being comes together and the richness of each current of ourselves can be maximized as we age. Perhaps it doesn't ever stop, which we will consider in the final part of this work.

4. Allowing Ourselves to Sleep

The natural regeneration time of our daily cycle is to sleep. To some extent it is a mystery why animals sleep and the professional literature offers many hypotheses. There is a significant disadvantage, for during sleep, you are vulnerable to harm. So, there must be a very important reason for sleep as part of our daily rhythm. I would posit that we have to dip into the currents of renewal operative in the universe and in our bodily fabric.

One can make the argument that consciousness that relies on so much expenditure of energy to the brain and neural activity needs the downtime to renew and regenerate itself. The same is also true for our two other evolutionary domains of mobility and sociality. We need more rest if we have long periods of physically exerting ourselves or after engaging in intense social activity.

There are periods where we may be driven by mission to keep lesser hours and ride the current or flow of energy that allows us to complete things. You can go with this flow. But the contrary tension is also present, that you will eventually need to recoup that expenditure. For all her mystical sayings, I recall one by St. Teresa of Avilla, in which she followed a bodily theology: "If you are hungry, eat. If you are tired, rest." Listening to the body is key to all this. Sometimes we ride the energy that leaves us with less sleep. Other times the body is demanding sleep, which we should obey, if possible.

Some have trouble and may even have a fear of sleeping. Falling asleep is like a letting go, a type of dying to the day. This touches upon a mystery that we need to let go in order to rest and renew. We can't renew if we just keep going in whatever stream of activity we find ourselves doing. Letting go of our day allows a new day to take form.

In maximizing our renewal experience of sleep, we need to be alert to habits which result in sleep deprivation. Activities that are addictive and keep us up later than we know we should, depriving us of sleep, end up cheating us of renewal and the usual freshness of the following day. Everyone will from time to time break their patterns of healthy living, but try not to institutionalize them.

Like in so many things, a tension in opposites is at play. We want to live, to be awake, to continue to experience things fully. But we must let go and die to the day, in order to renew. If we go without sleep, we become disoriented and crazy. Our natural balance requires sleep. But the irony is, we cannot grasp at sleep either. For if we try too hard to sleep, we may stay awake. Even in achieving sleep, we must go let go trying to sleep, in order to let this natural process happen.

One clue is to at each night offer up the day you have lived in some fashion. This offering is a type of prayer that in offering the day to the universe, lets go of the day. Then we will, the universe willing, awake to consciousness the next day.

One theory of interest in the scientific literature was an article that proposed we go through the evolutionary layers of consciousness as we wake, from a primal vertebrate being to human consciousness. Perhaps we also make this evolutionary descent as we go to sleep. Our son at 13 years old is very independent during the day, but at night he reverts back to being his younger age, when he embraces me and says "Good night, Dad. I love you." In our sleep we return to our primordial youth, which grants us the energy for our next day of being.

So let sleep be your friend, your partner in renewal as you live your life.

5. Keeping Old Friends

One thing that surprised me as I became older is that friends of many years may choose to drop away. I do not know if it is because I grew up as a Southerner, a people who are hard to make friends with, but once friends, they are loyal. Perhaps the Northeast is more transactional, and you are friends as long as someone is engaged in some practical mutual exchange.

Even family members who may also be friends drop off as their lives change. To some extent, it is inevitable that people in your life will no longer be present. They move away, marry a spouse who does not like you, become someone different, and your prior appeal as a friend has diminished. Yet loyalty has a claim and though you may not be as close as you once were, I believe in the loyalty of old friends.

There are many advantages to long-lasting loyalty. Someone you've known for many years connects to your historical self and knows you as you have once been and have changed. Having this sense of history, they can be *message bearers* to you, with a higher accuracy of perception and knowing how to advise you. There is a level of acceptance that has endured the passage of time. It gives the opportunity for the expression of love, which is not by its nature ephemeral or fickle. When we are truly loved, we bathe in a warmth of renewal and live longer.

I have such a friend with whom I collaborated with for many years and who was a friend along with his family for decades. Yet, and though there was not any significant event that would have caused a rupture, his friendship dropped off. It is now in my dreams where I encounter him and his family. But I think how even though occasional contact could be healing, the other party does not desire that. It is a mystery to me how a person can move on, despite the bonds of love. But the nature of friendship is voluntary, and ultimately, we must respect another's choice.

With events such as these, we realize the fragility of our relationships and the price for loving. We can choose not to love and isolate ourselves to protect ourselves from pain. Or we can love and experience love's pain, in which the other person can leave you hurt. But as the saying goes, better to have love and lost than not to love at all. As a counter, we can think of the many relationships which have persisted, despite obstacles.

The truth is that the definition of family and friends are those who hurt each other and forgive each other. We cannot expect that we will not be hurt. The truth is too, if we reject one another due to some hurt, years will pass and we may well forget the original hurt, or wonder how such a small thing became so large. It is a surprising irony that things relatively small can lead to a rupture in a relationship, such is the sensitivity and feelings involved when persons love another.

Relationships, if they are deep, have the capacity to hurt us. They also present the challenge of being able to forgive one another. Whole workshops and books are written on the topic of forgiveness. But one key to forgiveness is to have humility and realize that we, too, hurt others and are often not fully conscious of the hurt we dispense.

So, do old friends keep us young? Sometimes people who have known us for some time envision us a certain way and don't see us as different even though we have changed. That is a hazard, and perhaps those persons are ones who are more acquaintances than friends. For a true friend allows you to change, to become someone new, as you actualize your life.

6. Engage in Rituals of Renewal/Healing

The Scripture reading this Sunday, as I'm writing this work, was about the leper who is healed, his flesh becoming like that of a child. He did so by following the simple instruction to wash in the Jordan. This struck me as related to the theme of renewal, and that healing and rituals of healing are experiences of renewal. I once recovered from a long bout of bronchitis in which I felt deathly ill and had the sacrament of anointing for the sick/last rites. As I became well and the illness shed, I felt a great release, like being born to life again.

Spiritual rituals, almost by definition, are opportunities for renewal. In the Christian church, the sacraments of baptism, reconciliation, communion, and anointing of the sick can all be interpreted as granting us renewal. In early Christian baptismal imagery, nudity and using a child-sized figure to represent the baptized was an image of renewal, of dying and rising. In this sacrament, one was also cleansed from their failings/sin. This also recalls the process of reconciliation/confession, a sacrament neglected by most, in which sharing our failings/sin with another grants a powerful feeling of renewal.

To some extent the past accumulates, burdens us and makes us old. Periodically, we have to let go of the past, not be weighted down, so we can become new again. Rituals help this process to unfold. What rituals we employ to renew are what each of us must find. They may involve periods of vacation, which break up the pattern of our life and let something new emerge. It could even take a more focused form as a spiritual retreat. The first stage of retreat can be uncomfortable as difficult material we have shunted to the side surfaces. But the net effect of a successful retreat is to be renewed and refreshed. As such, we can experience a *positive withdrawal,* where we set aside the patterns of our living for a time in order for something new to emerge.

Renewal can come with a price, where we need to sacrifice something, do something we don't want to, but love demands that we do. I am thinking of penance and pilgrimages, in which we make a long trip to meet and honor the loved ones of our life. The ritual yearly trip to meet with a lifelong friend may fall into such a category. I have already mentioned the long trip I did not want to take, to see an ill friend in his later 80s. Yet I did so, and I found myself gifted and renewed. It turned out that he directed me to visit a friend's property in a remote area of Alabama, which became an adventure as I sensed a strong presence in at a monumental stone formation that looked like a human-bird form. It is an irony that doing the things we do not want to do can be the most life-giving.

This section challenges us to consider what rituals we have in place to renew, what new ones we need to seek, and to make use of them.

7. *Music as a Source of Renewal*

Part of my day has increasingly been to listen to music, especially by watching YouTube videos of singers or the various Voice contests. Though I don't play an instrument or have a particular skill with music, I enjoy entering into music deeply. Intuitively, I feel that music accesses a renewing energy within us.

One theory of the origin of speech places a musical type of communication prior to articulated words. Music touches a deep essence or soul within us, and perhaps it arises from the deeper aspects of our evolutionary self. It combines rhythm, which is an impulse to movement and dance, and melody which carries our feelings.

Music also features resonance, a full tonal quality which may be prolonged and amplified by other sounds. The full range of highs and lows are found in live music, versus recorded music which compresses the range of sound. The advantage of hearing live music is touted by websites such as *WindRiver,* as reducing stress, making us happy, increasing social connection, and slowing down aging.

Music, to me, is a mystery, how the three dimensions of word, rhythm and melody come together to create a flow upon which we travel. How is it that certain mathematical proportions of frequency create a scale with resonances that are pleasing to us? Perhaps it helps create a full alignment of our bodily energies or chakras. The mystery of vibration's impact on our soul and deeper self have probably not been fully explored, but it gives us cause to wonder.

Music is part of the shaman's equipment to enter into an altered state and experience trance. A constant rhythmic beating of drums or shaking a rattle, along with a stress posture, are sufficient to induce a trance state. Trance creates an unusual physiological response which combines an elevated heart rate with a drop of blood pressure, an emergency state of being. Here, one can access healing processes and ecstatic states. In one personal example, I was grieving the suicide of a poet friend of mine, and had tried a purification posture from a Southeast Ceremonial figurine. I experienced a type of vomiting up of black particles, as if the grief was leaving me, and I was left feeling purified. Subsequently, I went on to publish her poems in a small volume called *Walk in Beauty*.

Children naturally sing and many songs have a type of child-like rhythm and youthful tone to them. It's my intuition that music is a hidden source of renewal that we should all dip into, whose resonances bathe the body with youthful, healing energy.

8. Humor and Laughter

During this project I tell friends that I am writing a book, and I take their suggestions to heart. One friend of mine, Casey Downy, is 75 and an accomplished sculptor from Mobile, Alabama. He believes that the key to handling aging is humor. Intuitively, we sense that a person's ability to laugh at the world and themselves has a healthier perspective, which is not weighed down by the burden of years. Humor is lightness, and one feels their spirit rising within groups that laughs together.

Non-human primates, like chimpanzees, show laughter-like sounds during physical play. With rapid breathing sounds are made upon both inhalation and exhalation of breath. Younger babies also laugh upon inhalation and exhalation, but older babies and adult humans only laugh upon exhalation. What significance this has is conjectural, although I can see laughter as essentially a release, a letting go.

Another difference with humans is that we laugh during social interactions. This calls to mind laughter in my mind and friends with whom our conversation involves a deep laughter. I had good friends, George and Diana, who were like second parents to me in Baltimore, and I recall many times after dinner at their house when our laughter escalated to belly laughs. When we laugh together with others, we are experiencing a wellspring of youth. Typically, children are never far from joy and laughter, living on that edge. At Diana's Buddhist memorial service, I recalled this laughter, and how we experienced it as being one.

So let us try to laugh together. Perhaps we should consciously make the attempt when we are together with others. Laughter is infectious and it can open doors within others. When we laugh, we are young together again.

When we laugh at ourselves, we let go of ourselves. The walls of the ego crumble before laughter, and we realize our common humanity. Perhaps, at this point, love enters us more fully.

9. Positive Thinking

Related to humor is positive thinking. Some recent articles have suggested that keeping a positive attitude enhances longevity. This makes intuitive sense, for a negative attitude would ultimately be more stressful and depress the body's natural functions. A positive attitude is also more attractive socially, as people tend to aggregate more consistently around positive sources of energy.

This calls to mind a book written about a phrase from the Greek philosopher, Aristotle, *The Fragility of Goodness*. The dilemma we face in life can be framed this way. We try to do good; persons take advantage and do us harm, and we are challenged to keep doing good. A paradox within this is that the harm we encounter is often a valuable source of character formation, and makes for the drama of our lives.

Once, I wrote a resume of my failings, including a breakdown experience, lost jobs, and other things you would not put in a resume. Framed this way, it brought laughter. But it points to the reality that our life is littered with failings. Yet, we could do an opposite list of things of the good we have accomplished, barriers we have overcome, and the good we are still doing. They are our blessings. The positive person has a sense of this list ever before them. I gained this perspective, in part, from scripture, the prayer by Mary called the Magnificat. Here she praises God for tearing the high from their thrones and raising the lowly. This is the wild card of our lives. That no matter how low we have been, there is a vast heart beating in the universe that works to raise us up. Perhaps this is the greatest secret of the universe.

10. Our Hair, Our Face

Our hair and our face are something I have failed to mention, yet it is perhaps the most obvious indicator of aging. First, let's consider hair, which surrounds and highlights the face.

As we age, we lose the color in our head hair. A solution, of course, to those who would remove this sign of aging is to color your hair. This works relatively successfully, shaving off the appearance of several years. It can even be seen as a ritual of renewal, as many Indigenous rituals involve alteration to one's hair. Last, in a youth-oriented culture, it may reduce discrimination to a person based on their age.

However, the choice to color your hair is very individual. In my case, I have colored my hair a handful of times, something I no longer do. I jest to people that I have opted to keep a relatively young face with older looking hair, rather than young colored hair with an older face. To some extent, I felt that coloring is a denial of your age and risks an inauthentic presentation of self. In addition, I am wary of any hidden risk of chemicals entering the pores of my head. But that is just my decision, and I think there is value to going either way.

Cutting your hair and the length of hair is a second major decision with the appearance of your hair. In the case of men, it seems as you age, keeping your hair short makes you look younger. Unruly hair that has grown out of its haircut makes you look older. If the hair is uncolored, there is simply more gray. As a photographer I know that silver or white attracts the eye amid a darker surround, so it simply stands out more. In the case of an artist look, however, longer hair may also be a sign of youth and being carefree. Thus, what length you allow your hair to grow is also a decision that impacts your appearance as you age.

Last night I had a dream that involved the length of my hair and prodded me to do this section. In my dream I am at a university, researching an obscure mythic truth that is being kept hidden. As I go about the library, I discover my hair is in a ponytail, and I let it out. It is surprisingly long, nearly going down to my waist. Even more surprising is that a long length of it is a shiny brown. This is complemented by a strong streak intense white above. I interpret this to mean that I am finding ways to access youth, prodding by the writing of this work. The dream self did not erase all the white, however, and allowed a portion to be striking. It reminds me of women who may color their hair but leave a streak of white. Leaving the white in, I interpret, is a sign of wisdom and perhaps a bit of wizardry as well.

The dream, in which hair is at feminine length, reminds me of the Jungian concept that we incorporate more of the opposite sex in the second half of our lives. Thus, men are challenged to incorporate the feminine, rather than to simply progress in a linear fashion to a hyper-masculinity which becomes overbearing and oppressive. Likewise, women are challenged to incorporate the masculine dimension as they age, such as exerting a more active leadership in the social arena. In the trajectory of my life, I think I was more *being* oriented early on, and have moved toward a more active leadership/ mentorship role in my second half.

There remains the face, a critical aspect of our sense of self and perhaps most revealing in terms of our sense of, or status of, renewal. A face that shines, readily smiles and reveals emotion is considerably different from a face which is habitually dower, frowning, or cold. We might observe the face of children, which often has a sheen of joy and playful mirth. This is a moment we might consider our face and our demeanor, which shows and reveals the passage of years.

The face, interestingly, is a biological organ that develops uniquely in the fetus. The set of muscles present is amazingly complex and increasingly complexified in the three stages of primate evolution that led to humans. The active face may be overlooked, for we don't see ourselves as we express our emotion to others.

What makes the difference between a youthful face and one that looks old? We have already addressed the natural biological dimension, considered in our section on skin. We are advised not to overtreat the skin and to allow the natural biological flora to do its work. But what is the secret to a youthful face? A clue is found in the saying that the eyes are a window to the soul. In this sense our face with its demeanor is the most direct expression or indicator of our inner state. Thus, if our inner being is experiencing renewal, it will show in our face.

There is a saying of Jesus to the effect of how important inner states are, that those who look with hatred are in effect killing their own brother and sister. Perhaps those who would obscure their intentions have learned to be deadpanned, to have a poker face, to keep things close to the vest. This may develop so that you can manipulate others, but also to avoid being hurt by revealing too much. Either way, persons have found refuge in looking like a mannequin.

A sign of humanity is emotion, in particular empathic emotion, which shows we are feeling what the other person is expressing. C. S. Lewis has written a book, *Till We Have Faces*, suggesting that we come to have a face when we actualize our full humanity.

We don't try to renew inside in order to look youthful. We renew inside, for that is an inherent value and a natural object of our humanity. A side effect is that we will look more youthful to others.

PART VII
RENEWAL AND DEATH

One quote that I have cited to others in discussions about aging is a prayer by Teilhard de Chardin, which I paraphrase: "As we grow weaker and diminish, let our spirit grow stronger." Though this book has a strong subtheme of taking care of ourselves to increase longevity, at its heart is the theme of experiencing renewal as we age, for whatever amount of time we have.

Inevitably, unless there is sudden death, we will experience degrees of decline and loss of bodily function. By the time we enter the 80s or earlier, we come to periods of trial, where the challenge to renew becomes more acute and tested. I have not made this journey yet and perhaps can add that chapter if I live to that age. But now, I would like to think it is possible that renewal continues.

I would like to believe too that death is the last challenge of renewal, in which we birth, possessing an eternal consciousness. If what we experience throughout our life is any indicator of what will come, this can be viewed as a reasonable hope. Perhaps this is too big of a leap, for which we do not have much, if any, first-hand experience of the beyond.

Yet, persons who experience the death of another person can experience that death as life-giving. It has been my paradoxical experience that while attending my two sibling's deaths, the certitude of such a continuance became strongest. I don't know why that feeling and experience would come to me at this point. It is like the veil between worlds becomes thinner at death, encompassing persons around the dying person. We face the paradox and the possibility that experience of dying is that the person is being renewed, that he or she is transforming and entering another realm.

Experience during acts of love—in this case, attending to someone's death—do not lie. They are not offered here as a proof of afterlife.

Rather, they are offered as a shared life experience, from which each person can add their own experience, discernment, and reflection.

In the more immediate term, we are called to live as full a life of possible, a fullness that we acquire through ongoing renewal. Day by day, the inner person renews. Such is the life we are called to live and offer to others.

CONCLUSION

In one of my works, the *Mystery of Essences*, I imagined archetypal essences in the universe, which we can tap into. The Fountain of Youth was sought by Ponce de Leon in my birthplace of Florida, and I imagine this pilgrimage now as a search for such an essence.

Imagine there is an essence of renewal, whether it comes from a fountain of water or flame. How do we get close to this? In this work we have outlined many ways to dip into sources of renewal, whether it be by music, ritual, humor, or social connection. It gives us pause to meditate and reflect upon the activities that renew us, that make us feel young again.

In a sense our life journey is a search for youth and eternity, the continuance of life and meaning. Amazingly, we live like we will live forever, even when we are in our later years. We deny death because it does not seem right that it should be victor over our lives. St. Comboni, whose card I received last Sunday, gives us the saying, "I die, but my work will never die."

Our work does not stop in our later years. We do not retire, but begin new chapters. We live for eternity, and we die into eternity. Such is our final hope in aging and renewal.

Don't miss out!

Visit the website below and you can sign up to receive emails whenever Michael A. Susko publishes a new book. There's no charge and no obligation.

https://books2read.com/r/B-A-GJLJ-KRHBC

BOOKS 2 READ

Connecting independent readers to independent writers.

Did you love *Aging and Renewal: Living the Full Life*? Then you should read *The Meaning, Beauty & Mystery of Dreams: Seven Guidelines and Seven Tools for Listening*[1] by Michael A. Susko!

This work offers a guide that sums up years of dream interpretation. We are given both general guidelines on how to approach our dreams and specific tools to understand their symbolic significance. Each of these is illustrated by the author's own dream life. Not only will we discover how to find meaning in dreams, but we will come to see the value of their beauty and mystery. The net result is that we will become comfortable handling the dream world, and be led to awareness and actions that will help fulfill our lives. This fulfillment is in harmony with the personalized and universal aspiration that the dream world seeks to grant us.

Read more at https://www.allroneofus.com/.

---

1. https://books2read.com/u/4EJdP0

2. https://books2read.com/u/4EJdP0

Also by Michael A. Susko

A Couple Through Time
Down Below and the Archon's Castle
Up Above and the Runaway
Across the Gulf and Journey Into Un-Time
On the Bay and a Child Found
In the Wild and Do One Wild Thing
On the Mountain and Two Are Missing
To the Beginning and Journey Through Here

Archetypal Worlds
Alwon in Another World: An Archetypal Voyage
Line On the Wall
The Alien's Gift
The Gold People
Spider Woman and the Timeroc
Quill Ears & the Other Earth
Darkwood and Dual with the Shadow Side
Giant Under the Mountain

Early Humanity

The Firekeeper
Child of the Elements

Haikus and Photos
Flowers and Haikus
Haikus and Photos: Guatemalan Highlands
Haikus and Photos: Water Birds and Reflections
Haikus and Photos: Seasons of New River
Haikus and Photos: Yosemite Wilderness
Haikus and Photos: California Coast
Haikus and Photos: Canadian Rockies
Haikus and Photos: Hawaii's Exotic Landscapes
Haikus and Photos: Vienna, People with Buildings and Art
Haikus and Photos: Slovakian Castles and Hamlets
Haikus and Photos: Berlin, Light and Dark
Haikus and Photos: New Orleans, City of Immigrants
Haikus and Photos: Antietam Wind and Spirits
Haikus & Photos: Plant Abstractions
Haikus and Photos: Appalachian Beauty
Haikus and Photos: Urban Farm in Sandtown
Haikus and Photos: New York Heights and Ground

Little Lion
The Lion and the Chameleon
The Elephant and the Chameleons

Nature Haikus & Photos
Haikus and Photos: Butterflies and Flowers

Haikus and Photos: Presence at Penn Bluff
Haikus & Photos: Mystery Form at Penn Bluff
Haikus and Photos: Essences at Penn Bluff
Haikus and Photos: World Archetypes at Penn Bluff

The Dreaming Series
Sleek Back
Streak and Cave Bear Dreaming
Moby and Marsupial Mole Dreaming

The Dream World Trilogy
Delphi, the Time Thief, and the Dream World
Detinna and the Cave God
The Resistance & the Empire

Transformational Stories
Caseness and Narrative: Contrasting Approaches to People
Psychiatrically Labelled
Transformative Experiences, Psychiatric Research, and Informed
Consent
Transformational Stories: Voices for True Healing in Mental Health

Writings from Street People
Street Images
Street Images II

About the Author

The author, holding degrees in philosophy and psychology, brings an interdisciplianry awareness to troubleshooting problems that arise as we age. His studies include publishing in the fields of biology, psychology, and indigenous studies. Perhaps more importantly he has aged and continues to be active in sports and raising his teenage son.

Read more at https://www.allroneofus.com/.

About the Publisher

AllrOneofUs Publishing seeks out work which will make a novel and qualitative addition to the world literature, and one that will last across generations. Many of these persons are in the later part of their life and have made exemplary contributions which are unrecognized. To cite a few examples, we recommend Rich Mullin's *Ethics and the Full-breasted Richness of Life*, John Susko's *Flowers of the Night: Musings from a Sentimental Son,* and Dr. Curtis Adams' *Psychosis and the Humpty Dumpty Story.*

9 7 9 8 2 1 5 2 9 9 3 6 4